SRI KSETRA
& Modern Pyay

Introduction by
Patrizia Zolese

Texts by
Michele Romano
Massimo Morello

Photos by
Andrea Pistolesi

Project Supervision by
Mauro Cucarzi

INTRODUCTION
by Patrizia Zolese

The images captured by Andrea Pistolesi, of an unusual landscape of the precious archaeological and monumental heritage of Myanmar, suggested the initiative. To present to a wider public a little known aspect of the history of urbanization in Southeast Asia: the cities of the Pyu culture.
The study on the emergence of cities and large religious centers is one of the hardest fields of historical and archaeological research because it requires the collection of a large amount of data, involving different sciences such as economy, trade, political change on a small and large scale, technology, territorial organization.
The research for what is commonly called the "state formation", ruled by a centralized power, oligarchy or theocracy, requires a holistic approach, that is, an open systemic vision which takes into account complex interrelationships, economic, social, and religious, and the causes that have produced them.
This means attempting to disentangle a plot of variability involving the exploitation and market requirements of natural resources (metals, spices, agricultural products, etc.), the opening of new trade routes over long and short distances by land or by sea, the birth or the decline of policies internal and external to the country, population growth, high-impact events such as wars, invasions, migrations and new alliances.
The reconstruction of the natural environment and territorial changes caused by nature, such as changes in the course of rivers and sea coasts or micro climate change, which determine the appearance or disappearance of flora and fauna, is another integral part of historic study to find evidence able to formulate an exhaustive picture of the transition from a village economy to the emergence of one or more socio-administrative centers: the city.
The birth of a city coincides often with the advent of writing - a necessary tool for administrative control to store business transactions and financial statements of a "multi-skilled" society or "urban society"'.
The urban society is composed of different and stratified working classes: artisans, merchants, soldiers, bureaucrats, farmers and so on, able to manage and organize villages, suburbs, agricultural and industrial areas, roads, canalization and infrastructure in general, surrounding the cities.
The written sources, both vernacular and imported, Sanskrit and Pali, in the case of ancient Myanmar, were drawn up in perishable material, such as dried palm tree leaves or carved on stone slabs, mainly reporting religious texts, genealogical and royal edicts.
The peculiar climatic conditions of the sub-tropical areas that favor the perishable nature of brittle materials and fires both accidental and induced, have resulted in an almost complete loss of those texts that could have been of great support for the reconstruction of civil society customs and the culture of many civilizations of southeast Asia.
The surviving stone inscriptions are limited in number and content, and the inscriptions provide elements too circumstantial to define a broad framework on the complexity of the political, cultural and everyday life of urban societies.

Temples and centers of thought have largely survived in comparison with the rapid disappearance or change of the city: the continuity of religious belief has allowed the preservation and maintenance of structures, as in the case of Bagan and Angkor.

For this reason, the commitment undertaken by the Government of Myanmar and UNESCO to safeguard the remains of the Pyu city takes on a double meaning: to protect important evidence and to preserve an immense cultural heritage for future scientific research, involving scholars of different disciplines for decades.

Since 2002, the Italian Archaeological Mission of the Lerici Foundation (Polytechnic of Milano), supported by the Italian Ministry of Foreign Affairs has collaborated with the Department of Archaeology, Museums and Libraries of the Ministry of Culture of Myanmar, for the scientific and technical training of officials and researchers, for the constant updating of the methodologies of conservation, excavation and study of the great cultural heritage of Myanmar.

In 2005 on the initiative of the Lerici Foundation and UNESCO, the Ministry of Culture of Myanmar has set up the Field School Of Archaeology (Pyay), an essential tool to ensure permanent courses, where local and foreign researchers teach the new generations of officials and postgraduate students.

In 2012, UNESCO, with the support of the Italian Government, promoted a project entitled "Capacity building for safeguarding Cultural Heritage in Myanmar" aimed at having the Pyu Cities and monumental complex of Bagan named as UNESCO World Heritage Sites.

We hope that the images published on this journey in the ancient city of Sri Ksetra, and those of the Pyay new city, representing a living sample of cultural and religious traditions, still maintaining ancient memories, will stimulate the interest of first-time visitors to Myanmar and those returning again to this country, still rich in atmospheres, customs and traditions, so rare in the context of Southeast Asia.

Pyu Culture

"The area of Pyu Kingdom is 3000 li from east to west and 5000 li from south to north. On the east it adjoined Khmerland of Cambodia, on the southeast Monland of Dvaravati (Old Siam), on the west India, on the north Nanchao and on the south the sea." (Translation from Chinese text; Tang period (7th – 9th cent. AD) - Nai Pan Hla, 2011)

In the first centuries of the Christian era, in upper Myanmar, we found the earliest manifestation of urban culture from anywhere in Southeast Asia.
From Chinese texts – mostly concerning the Tang period (7th – 9th century AD) we know that, at least from the 2nd century AD an urban society appeared in the upper part of the Ayeyarwady valley. This society was formed by a Tibeto – Burman group whose original name is unknown. Through the Chinese texts we have now named this urban culture Pyu, whose meaning in Chinese varied from "rebel" to "cavalry".
The main archaeological evidences of this culture consist in the remains of the three ancient capitals of Halin, Beikthano and Sri Ksetra, located close to the Ayeyarwady river, that clearly show the urban character of Pyu society.
The architectural features, the use of bricks and the design of gateways and religious buildings are common to all such three sites.
The three capitals are characterized by huge brick walls surrounding the city area. Inside and outside the walls there is a multitude of brick structures, mostly Buddhist and funerary buildings, together with constructions probably meant to have administrative purposes (i.e. the central palace – citadel laid in the centre of the city area).
Pyu cities showed impressive hydraulic systems. Using canals, moats and dams, the inhabitants were able to exploit the tributary rivers of the Ayeyarwady, in order to carry out agricultural development.
Another feature of the Pyu sites is the presence in the archaeological material of decorated burial urns, coins, bricks with finger marks and semi – precious beads. The presence of objects such as coins and beads underlines the connection between the Pyu cities and the neighbouring countries within a wider trade network linking China and India.

"They traffic with the neighbouring tribes in river-pigs (dolphins?), silk-cotton cloth, glazedware and earthen jars." (Translation from Chinese text; Tang period (7th – 9th cent. AD) - Nai Pan Hla, 2011)

Finally, the presence of a writing system and monumental statuary confirms, undoubtedly, the high degree of civilization attained by the Pyu culture.
Many scholars suggested a "sequence of capitals" paradigm, which means that each capital collapsed before the birth of the next one. At the same time it was commonly accepted that the rise of the city of Pagan (9th century AD) marks the abandonment of the Pyu cities.
Recent archaeological data, nevertheless, show that the Pyu centres coexisted in upper Myanmar for centuries and continued to survive even after the growth of Pagan.

ANCIENT
SRI KSETRA

BY MICHELE ROMANO

BEBE PAGODA

THE ANCIENT CITY

The name of Sri Ksetra, which in Sanskrit means *noble field*, is used in the Chinese sources to indicate the main city of the Pyu culture. Although there is no direct inscriptional evidence, Sri Ksetra is nowadays identified as being close to the modern city of Pyay.
In fact, here, there are the remains of the largest brick-walled site in all Southeast Asia (about 1450 hectares) and the huge quantity of vestiges undoubtedly confirms the Pyu presence in the area.
The richness of the material found and the large quantity of brick structural remains (more than 270) suggest the economic importance of Sri Ksetra for many centuries.
The use of brick as a construction material indicates the development of the Pyu society. This durable material was used mostly for religious monuments, but also for the enceinte and for hydraulic works. Furthermore, many of the bricks used show finger marks and, sometimes, numbers and letters on the surface, showing a well-organized production system.
As usual in all the societies of Southeast Asia, the majority of the buildings were in bamboo or wood – as nowadays – and there are no remains of such constructions recovered during excavations.
Unfortunately the lack of satisfactory stratigraphy analysis during past excavations does not allow us to pinpoint an exact chronology for Sri Ksetra. Nevertheless the currently accepted chronological range (5th – 9th centuries AD) could probably be extended at both ends.

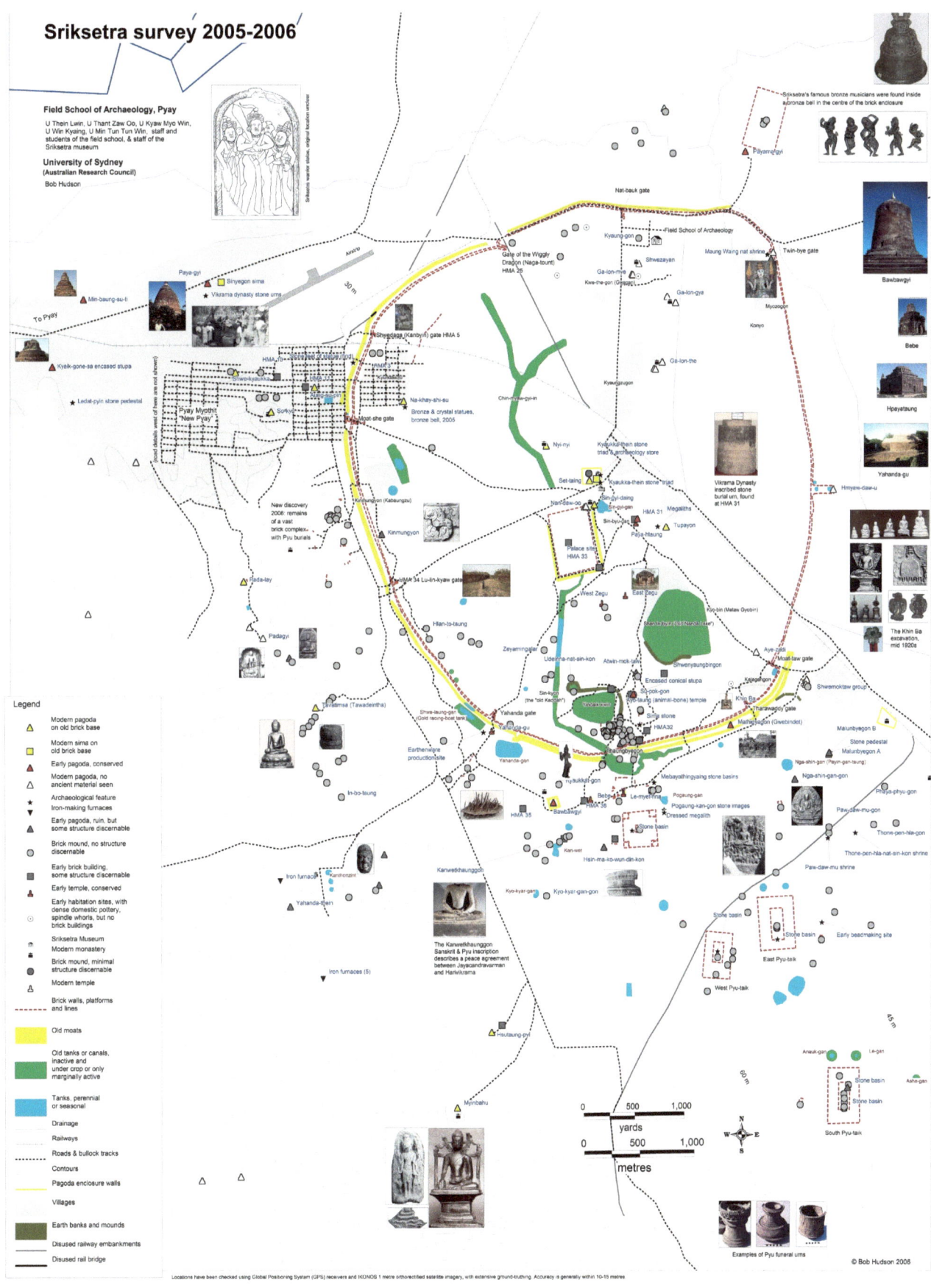

SRI KSETRA SURVEY 2005 – 2006 (*courtesy of Prof. Bob Hudson*)

NATPAUK GATE

LONG IRON NAILS FROM THE CITY WALLS

THE CITY WALLS

"The Pyu city has 12 gates with pagodas at the four corners. All the inhabitants live inside. For house building, they use timber and they make tiles of lead and tin for roofing" (Translation from Chinese text; Tang period (7th – 9th cent. AD) - Nai Pan Hla, 2011)

Sri Ksetra is enclosed by a massive brick wall with a roughly circular shape, while the other two Pyu cities have approximately rectangular enceintes.
Although the wall is related to the Pyu period, it is obvious that the contemporaneous shape came after centuries of alterations and restorations. Around the wall there are, nowadays, several openings, but only nine are identified as gates of the Pyu period, thanks to their particular shapes. The main gateways are characterized by an inward-turning corridor with alcoves. This kind of buildings may have an administrative function, or at least the intention to regulate the flow of people and to post personnel for controlling goods. (Hudson, 2004)

"The compass of the city wall is faced with glazed bricks: it is 160 li in circumference. The banks of the moat too are faced with bricks" (Translation from Chinese text; Tang period (7th – 9th cent. AD) - Nai Pan Hla, 2011)

The defensive purpose alone is not enough to justify the magnitude of this building and the functions of such a colossal enceinte are numerous. Meter – long nails were located in the wall, between the bricks and probably with a symbolic protective purpose. This fortification was also used for the regulation of water flow, but it should be considered that the wall may also have had a cosmological meaning and could be more an assertion of power made by the rulers.
In any case, once again, the magnitude of this structure underlines the high grade of work specialization of the Pyu society.

LULINKYAW GATE

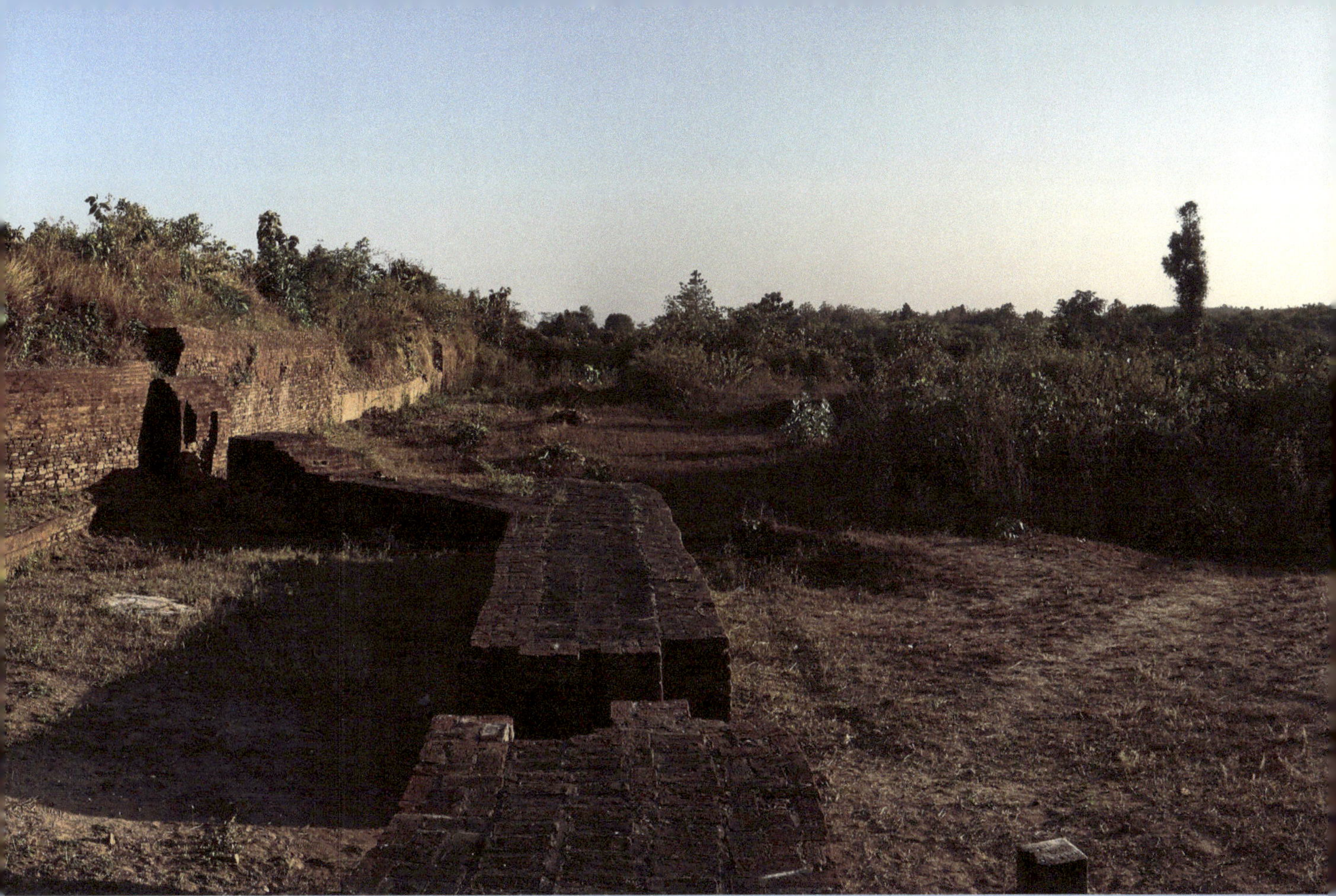
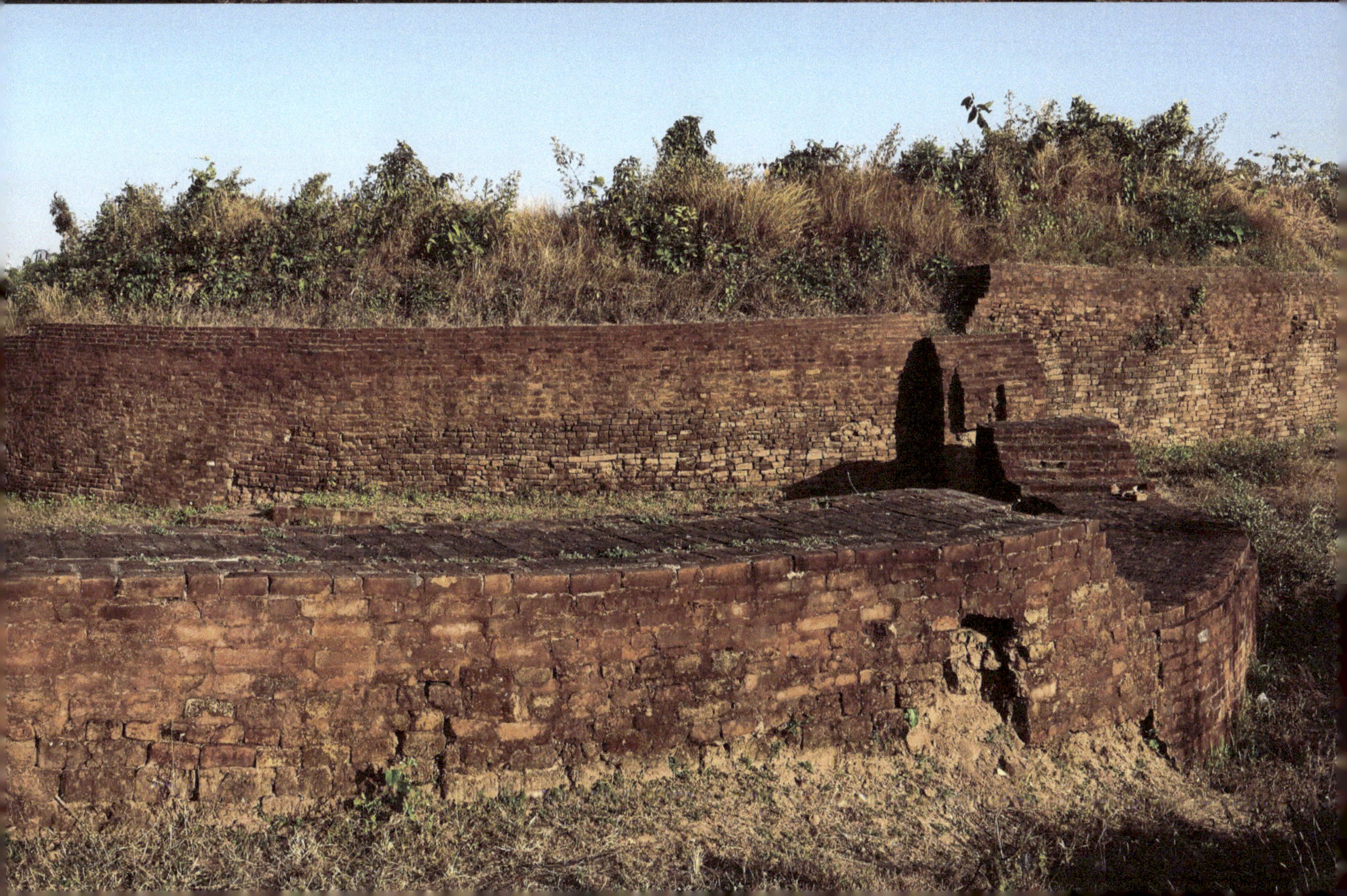

THE STUPAS

"There are over a hundred Buddhist monasteries with courts and rooms all decked with gold and silver, coated with cinnabar and bright colours, smeared with kino and covered with embroidered rugs" (Translation from Chinese text; Tang period (7th – 9th cent. AD) - Nai Pan Hla, 2011)

The Stupa is an architectural structure originally built by the first Buddhist worshippers to enshrine the relics of the Buddha Sakyamuni himself.

The first stupas, now disappeared, were simply earthen mounds, similar to the traditional prehistoric burial structures. After the death of Sakyamuni, they were built in India, close to the most significant place related to the Buddha life.

With the spread of Buddhism, starting in particular under the reign of King Asoka (3rd century BC), thousands of Stupas were built in all Asia. Stone and bricks started to be used for the construction of the stupas and the shape of these reliquaries started to be different from one region to another. Despite that, the Stupas have some common characteristics. They are composed by a dome, surrounded by a square base and surmounted by a pole with umbrella or parasols. In the centre of the base, in line with the central axis of the structure there is the reliquary where the relics (scale models of Stupa in precious materials, parts of the body or the clothes belonging to saint monks, sacred texts etc…) were placed.

The symbolism of the stupa is a vast and complex subject and every element has different meanings, but in general it underlines the presence of Buddha.

Synthetically, it is possible to consider the dome as the representation of Nirvana, the square base as the strong discipline necessary to reach enlightenment while the umbrella, symbol of royalty, recalls the royal lineage of Sakyamuni.

Another interpretation underlines the relation between the shape of the Stupa and the representation of Mount Meru, the holy place where the Gods live, according to Hindu culture.

In addition to the original symbolic and commemorative function, the construction of stupa also has many other meanings, including the purification of the land, the celebration of important events for the community and marking the main religious and communication routes (Snodgrass, 1985).

Just outside the wall of Sri Ksetra, three standing stupas mark the South, Northeast and Northwest of the city.

The Bawbawgyi stupa, located on the South, is 46 m high and is almost cylindrical, while, the Payagyi and the Payama stupas, respectively facing the Northwest and the Northeast, have been described as "sugarloaf" shaped. All the Stupas are made of brick, characterized by vertical cuts, probably for a better adhesion of the plaster. Anyhow, nowadays, only the brick surface is visible, while the plaster and the paint have completely disappeared.

It has been suggested that these buildings guarded the city from a cosmological point of view, but it is also very likely that they marked the main roads going into and out of the city. At the same time, it is not possible to define the exact chronology of these structures. Starting from a comparison of the shape with other stupas, mainly in India, some authors attribute these buildings to the 5th – 6th century AD.

BAWBAWGYI STUPA

PAYAMA STUPA

RELIQUARIES

PAYAGYI STUPA

PAYAGYI STUPA

BAWBAWGYI STUPA

BAWBAWGYI STUPA

EARLY PAGODAS

According to many scholars, within the total of 277 buildings of Sri Ksetra, approximately 65 ruins have been identified as structures belonging to a later period than the one presumed for the wall or the Stupas. Among these there are several rectangular Buddhist pagodas, made of brick, similar to those appeared in Pagan from the 9th – 10th century.
Some authors suggest that these buildings are prototypes of the Pagan one, but it is possible that they show how the Pyu occupation continued even after the rise of Pagan. Many of these pagodas, like Bebe or Lemyethna, also contain sculptures and reliefs older than the buildings. It is possible that the statues were relocated from other sites or probably they belonged to an earlier structure, renovated during the Pagan period.
Of these pagodas, Lemyethna, Bebe, Yahanda and East Zegu are the best preserved. They are characterized by a square sanctum (about 8 m each side) with a porch and they are surmounted by receding terraces with a cylindrical pinnacle on the top.
The side walls are decorated with pilasters and false doors. The presence of these kinds of pagoda mark another step in the evolution of Buddhism. They are temples, and through one or more doors, the believers could go inside to worship the stone images of Buddha.

EAST ZEGU PAGODA

BEBE PAGODA

BEBE Pagoda

Pyu Society

Sri Ksetra
MUSEUM

by Michele Romano

BUDDHISM

"They are delighted in the Buddhist laws. They wear gold-flowered hats and caps of kingfisher feathers strung with various jewels. The King's palace has two bells, one of silver and one of gold. When enemies are at hand, they burn incense and strike these bells. Thus obtaining omens concerning their fate in the coming battle. There is a great Buddha image, white in colour, 100 ft high in front of the palace." (Translation from Chinese text; Tang period (7th – 9th cent. AD) - Nai Pan Hla, 2011)

According to the tradition, after the death of Buddha Sakyamuni (about 5th century BC), his body parts were located, as relics, in the first stupas, close to key places in Buddha's life.
The monks and the followers used to move from one stupa to another to worship the Buddha relics and so, from the very beginning, the spread of Buddhism doctrine was encouraged.
Starting from the 3rd century AD, thanks to the activity of King Asoka and his successors, Buddhism knew a period of great expansion across the entire Indian continent reaching the Indo-Greek region of Ghandara and Kashmir in the North.
Buddhism was born out of oral tradition and the first monasteries were built along the main trading routes for sheltering the itinerant monks during the rainy season. Starting from the 1st century AD, with the appearance of the first written text, the monasteries grew to become important centres of instruction all over Asia.
Over the centuries many currents have been developed, but it is possible to divide Buddhism into two main schools: Mahayana and Theravada.

Buddha Image Carved In Terracotta

Buddha Images Carved In Sandstone Slabs

The latter, born in Sri Lanka in the 3rd century AD, arrive in Myanmar probably at the time of King Asoka, but, officially, the king of Pagan adopted Theravada Buddhism only in the 11th century. Starting from the 13th century, Buddhism disappeared from India. In the meanwhile, the doctrine had been carried to Southeast and East Asia, where it remains strong to this day in several different forms.

In the Pyu cities the strong presence of Buddhist images and monuments confirms the spread of Buddhism in Myanmar even before the rise of Pagan. Furthermore, many of the Buddhist reliefs found in Sri Ksetra present inscriptions in Pyu language. The Pyu script was used mostly for religious and royal purposes. It is a sophisticated Brahmi-derived language and it is not yet totally translated.

Amongst the archaeological finds, the numerous votive tables found testify to the strong activity of Buddhist worshippers in Pyu society.

Even if they were an image offered by the pilgrims to the monastic community or a sort of souvenir given to the worshippers, the votive tablets are one of the portable objects moving along the trade routes. Their presence as well as the large number of sculptural images and inscriptions found at Sri Ksetra confirms, once again, the high degree of civilization achieved by the Pyu culture and the key role of the Pyu cities in the network of the first urban societies of Southeast Asia.

Terracotta Votive Tablets

CREMATION

The Pyu used to burn their dead and store their ashes in burial urns. These urns were then placed in extensive cemeteries that have been found during the excavation both inside and outside the city walls.
The practice of cremation, with the deposition of the ashes and bones in urns, is probably a prehistoric tradition that continued even after the development of the Buddhist cult.
In the Pyu cities these urns appear inside or near Buddhist structures. They are often unglazed, made of common red ware and sometimes feature decorations. Inside the urn a small iron rod is frequently deposed which, as seen before for the iron nails in the wall, has a protective meaning.
For the ruling elite, stone urns could be used instead of ceramic ones. At Sri Ksetra, in the early 20th century, five stone urns with inscriptions were found. These inscriptions contain the names of at least six kings – characterized by the Sanskrit morpheme –vikrama, which means strong or heroic - that ruled the city probably from the late 7th to the early 8th centuries.
The stone burial urns of Sri Ksetra are, nowadays, the only evidence of a period of dynastic continuity in the Pyu cities.

Sandstone Burial Urns

Carved Sandstone Slabs That Covered The Relic Chamber Of Khin Ba

Charles Duroiselle

Charles Duroiselle was a famous epigrapher, expert in Pali language, who in 1906 wrote a grammar that is still in use today (A Practical Grammar of the Pali Language).
In the decades that followed, between 1912 and 1940, as Superintendent of the Archaeological Survey of Burma, Charles Duroiselle excavated at least 120 monuments in Myanmar. The acquisition of sculptures, statues and inscriptions was recorded in the annual reports.
In 1926 Charles Duroiselle performed an excavation in the Khin Ba stupa (already in ruin) and he excavated the remains of the relic chamber still not looted by treasure hunters. The treasure was found covered with two carved sandstone slabs. The relic chamber was well documented at the time, despite the characteristic inattention to stratigraphy and to the general condition of the monuments.

As Duroiselle wrote in his report:
"The most numerous and important finds during the year under report were those made at a site known as the Khin-bha-gon, near the Kalagangon village in the neighbourhood of Hmawza (Sri Ksetra). They consist of sculptures and ornamental pieces in burnt clay and sandstone, many small stupas and Buddha images in gold and silver, inscriptions on gold and silver plates, coins, crystal, jade and glass beads etc…"
(Archaeological Survey of India, 1926, pp. 171 – 176)

Anyhow, even if some objects have been attributed to the 5th century AD, it is possible that the monument may have been repaired and re-dedicated with some additions over the centuries.

Khin Ba Mound in 1926
Before The Excavation Of Charles Duroiselle

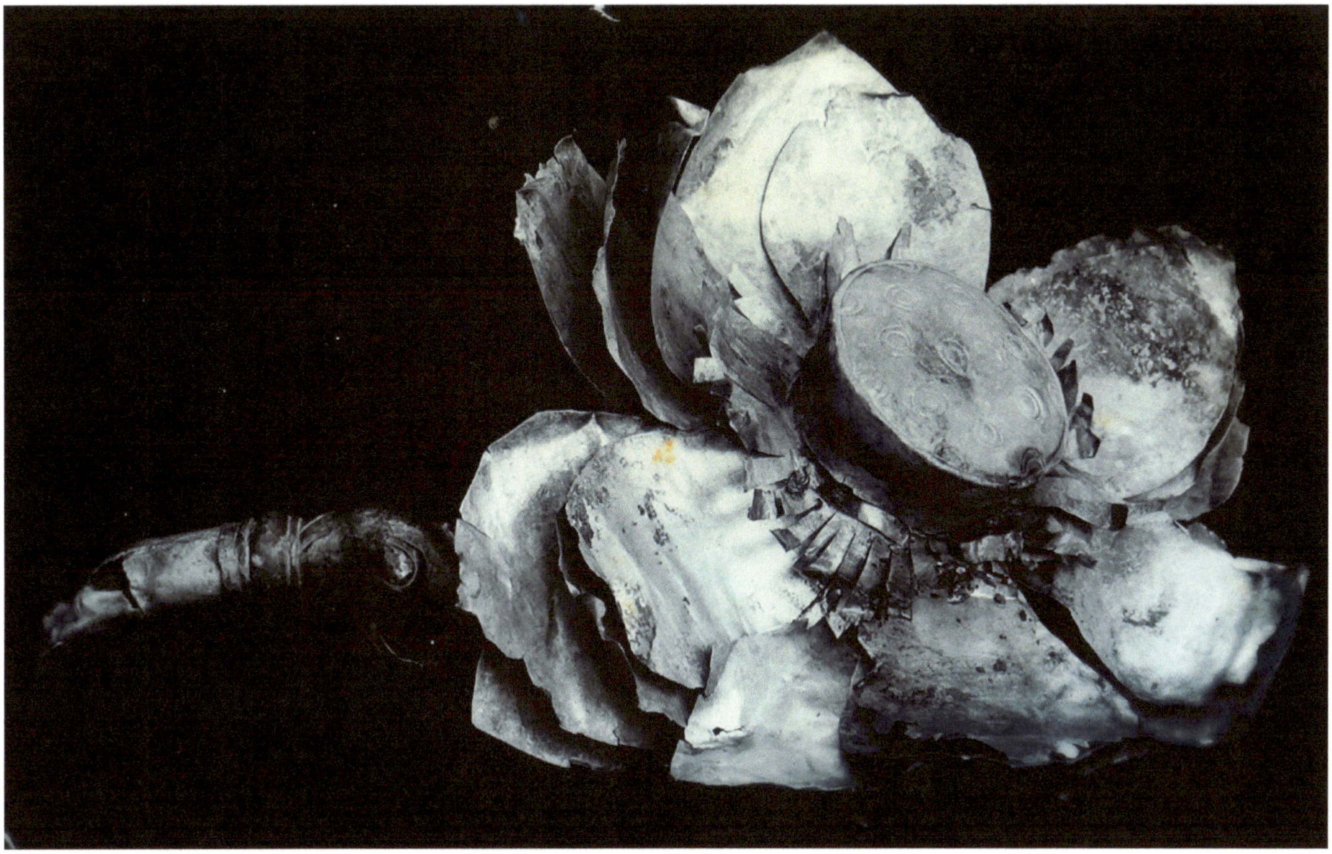

SILVER LOTUS FLOWER AND SILVER GILT STUPA
FROM THE RELIC CHAMBER OF KHIN BA

Training course in Archaeological site conservation

Between October and December 2012, in the framework of the "Capacity Building for Safeguarding Cultural Heritage in Myanmar" project, a team from the Italian institute Lerici Foundation set off to train local and national functionaries.
The mission based itself at the Pyay Field School of Archaeology, situated some 6 kilometres outside the town of Pyay and just outside the northern gate of the walls of the ancient town of Sri Ksetra and, during the three months lectures were given and on-site sessions conducted.
In the framework of this project the Department of Archaeology of Myanmar expressly selected Khin Ba site as the training course for demonstrating excavation methodology.
Despite the importance of the treasure, little is known about the architecture of the stupa and no studies have been carried out on its context. Duroiselle's excavation was performed to verify the existence of the relic chamber, and since the monument is partially collapsed, the removal of the brick debris was done quickly, collecting only some of the terracotta antefix decorating the outer sides of the monument.

As mentioned before, the reports delivered by the excavator left poor description about the area condition at his arrival, (how large was the area covered by collapsed structures? Was the collapse due to abandonment? What was the brick masonry of the chamber like? Were any of the walls of the presumed platform still standing?) . The importance of the discovery, also in terms of gold or silver value, soon attracted the interest of treasure hunters, who according to the officials of the Department of Archaeology (Myanmar), conducted an intense activity of looting, quite uninterrupted, from the '30s until the '80s. This activity aimed to find any other hidden treasures or carvings still uncovered.

When the area was definitively left (even complete bricks were stolen to be reused in surrounding villages) the area was overgrown by intense vegetation (including trees) growing on the site and on the craters left by the looters.

Although this is not the right context to describe all the data collected during the training course, the excavation was able to rehabilitate an area abandoned to nature and, most of all, to recover elements able to provide information about the dimension and the architectonic character of the monument housing such important relics.

After three months of archaeological and topographical activities within an area of about 1000 sqm it was possible to figure out a plausible architectonic model of the Khin Ba stupa.

Terracotta Antefix Recovered By Duroiselle In 1926

Detail Of The Carved Sandstone Slabs That Covered The Relic Chamber Of Khin Ba

WHERE THE OLD FLOTILLA LAY

"There he boarded a small steamer of the Irrawaddy Flotilla Company...He had noticed little in Prome, only some crumbling ruins and a bustling market by the port. Now on the river, he felt a lightening, a separation from the hot crowded street of Rangoon, of the delta..." This is how Prome appeared to the protagonist of "The Piano Tuner", a novel by Daniel Mason set in 1886, at the time of the third Anglo-Burmese War.

The names have changed. Prome is Pyay and the Irrawaddy is now the Ayeyarwady. The Irrawaddy Flotilla Company steamers (at that time the largest Company in the world in river transportation), which shuttled back and forth between what was then Rangoon and Mandalay up to Bhamo, are now out of commission.

But along that stretch of river, along the middle path of the Irrawaddy valley, the landscape is the same as that which inspired Rudyard Kipling's verses, strangely potent in their evocation:

"Come you back to Mandalay,
Where the old Flotilla lay:
Can't you 'ear their paddles chunkin' from Rangoon to Mandalay?
On the road to Mandalay,
Where the flyin'-fishes play".

Those scenes can also be rediscovered amongst maritime archives, in museums and antiquarian libraries: journals and travel tales noted down by British officers and bureaucrats. It's the kind of research conducted by the likes of Mauro Cucarzi of the Lerici foundation, one of those leading the archaeological studies in Pyu cities. It was he, in one of those conversations in which history blends into a story, that mentioned the Irrawaddy Flotilla: how, while strolling along the river near Pyay, he could visualise the stories described in the books of old.

The landscape around Pyay is thus evocative of a literary landscape. This happens because it is "a historical landscape". This time the definition comes from Patrizia Zolese, the archaeologist leading the research. "The importance of the Pyu sites is that they are part of a historical landscape. The ancient landscape is still here: the monuments, the ecosystem, the life itself in a certain sense."

In other words, the Pyay region is a map of Burmese history. For Patrizia, this leads back to the core of her studies: "How are cities born? Why does a village grow into a city?"

Yet, taking into account this space-time mechanism, all of this gives another dimension to the landscape. The monks, standing in long lines for the morning alms collection under the riverside trees or between the canals criss-crossing the fields dotted with stupas, follow in the footsteps of their predecessors, who made this territory one of the cradles of Theravada Buddhism in the 4th century. The irrigation systems and wells that still feed these lands in the Dry Zone, enabling the cultivation of rice and flowers, are the same as those in the ancient Pyu kingdoms. And amongst the flower pickers, often dressed to match the colour of the petals, you could almost glimpse Kipling's "Burma girl".

COUNTRYSIDE AND SPIRITS

Following the Ayeyarwady south of Pyay, the right-hand river bank, where a cliff drops into the water, is populated by hundreds of Buddhas. They observe the river from niches in the stone: large, small, in different postures, white, colourful, some rough-hewn, others as pristine as in a temple. The place is called Akauktaung and reaching it still provides the thrill of a little, mysterious adventure.

At the time of the Irrawaddy Flotilla, towards the end of the second Anglo-Burmese War, this was the borderline between the territories occupied by the British and those governed by the Burmese King. And this is where the steamers had to stop to pay a toll. Which explains the name of the place, which means "Toll hill". It also explains the Buddhas. The boatmen and sailors sculpted them to kill time during the long delays and, at the same time, as a way of appealing for good sailing – whirlpools are frequent on that stretch – and good business.

During the rainy season, many images are partly submerged, resulting in a kind of small-scale Burmese Atlantis. All reappear on the riverbank during the dry, hot season. Any season is good for disembarking and climbing up the thousand or so steps leading to the pagoda at the top of Akauktaung.

Above the river, amongst the trees, you meet other characters from the mystical Burmese world. Or, rather, the underworld. They are the Nats, or Spirits, the witnesses of the animistic cults predating Buddhism and which the latter has assimilated. They are found in the Nat Kon, or little altars, niches set into the tree or actual little houses at the foot of the centuries-old trunks of the sacred fig tree, decorated with red and white ribbons. According to tradition, there are 36 of them (the 37th being considered the Buddha), but every territory adds its own, making up a pantheon of popular religion. They are local characters that in life were famous, loved or feared and that often suffered a violent death. They then became spirits watching over a specific family, village or social group, and are honoured and revered to ensure they remain benevolent instead of transforming into vindictive ghosts.

The cult is particularly widespread along the Ayeyarwady river, especially in the more isolated rural areas such as Pyay. Where a Nat Pwe, or feast of the spirits, is celebrated almost every day. Bring a flower if you want to attend.

Pyay

BY MASSIMO MORELLO

THE BUDDHA'S PROPHECY

It is said that the Buddha stopped to meditate on a hill overlooking what would become Pyay ("Capital"). Here he prophesied the construction of a pagoda in that very place.

The prophecy, according to other legends, came true in the year 589 before the Common Era at the hands of two merchant brothers with the support of the Kings of the Dragons, the Orks and the Deva, the Hindu-Buddhist angels. Legend has it that four curls from the Buddha's head are housed within the zedi (stupa). Which explains the name of the pagoda: Shwesandaw, or Golden Hair Relics.

Since then it has become one of Burma's most sacred places, regularly renovated by those ruling over the city in order to benefit their own karma. The first was King Duttabaung - the founder of Sri Ksetra, he extended the construction to its current size and appearance. Thirty-nine metres tall (almost 89 from the bottom of its steep staircase), it is surrounded by 64 smaller pagodas. Its distinguishing feature, unique in all of Burma, are its two umbrellas atop the zedi: the first dates back to the Pyu era, while the second was installed by King Bamar Alaungpaya when he gained control of the city in 1754 CE. Then and now, it is considered a symbol of unity amongst the various Burmese ethnicities. But perhaps also of domination (the umbrella on top belongs to the conqueror), if not of the fear of disturbing a mystical layout. In that sense, the Burmese governors have always been very cautious.

At the south-west corner of the complex, Shwesandaw houses another relic: one of the Buddha's teeth. It is the non-authentic duplicate of the one preserved in Kandy, in Sri Lanka. Having been placed beside the original tooth-relic of Kandy for a time it is believed to have absorbed the aura of the original and become just as potent. The tooth-relic is customarily taken out of its chamber in the month of Dazaungmone (November-December) every year and ceremoniously taken on a tour of the city once every three years so that worshippers may pay homage to it and revere it with their own eyes.

Finally, looking east from Shwesandaw, you'll see an enormous seated Buddha figure rising up from the treeline. This is the statue dominating the Sehtatgyi Paya (Big Ten-Storey Buddha). It is strange to look a prophecy in the face.

SHWESANDAW PAGODA

SHWESANDAW PAGODA

Archaeological Gallery In The Old Public Library In Pyay

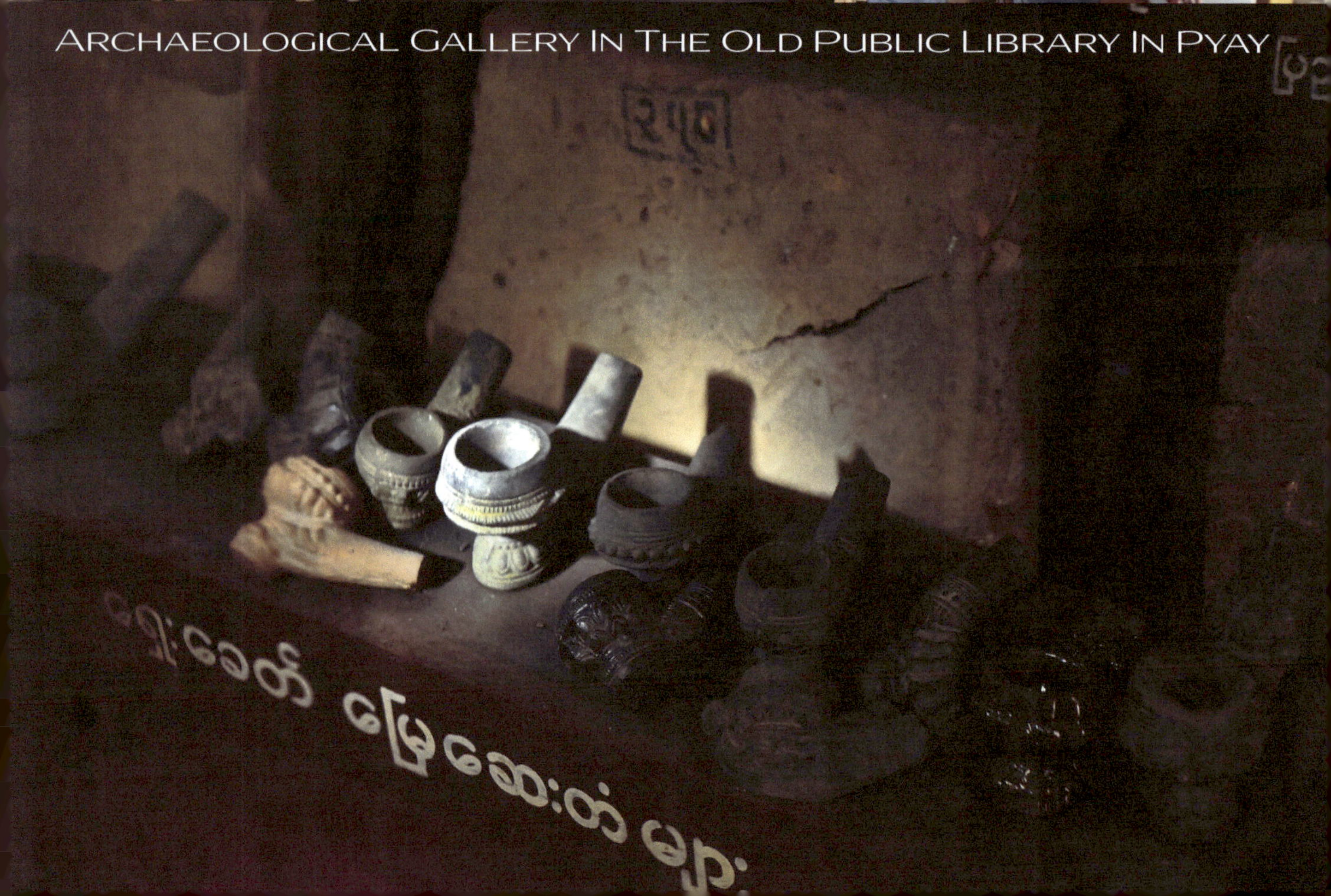

BACK TO THE PAST

"Prome…Blue-books describe annually the progress it has made along the path of civic virtue, and long pages record its statistics to some unknown end…" So wrote V.C. Scott O'Connor, who served in Burma as a British colonial officer, in the precious book "Mandalay and Other Cities of the Past of Burma" (Hutchinson & Co., London, 1907). At that time the city was called Prome - a mispronunciation of the town's Burmese name, Pyay. It had a population of 30,000 and, by all the standards of the age, could be considered an important centre. "It is equipped with a Municipality, a Jail, a Court House, Waterworks, and various other blessings of the kind commonly provided by a conscientious, hard-working, tax-collecting Government".

Some time later, in the '20s, Prome was described by Thant Myint-U in "The River of Lost Footsteps" as *"…a pleasant place, with handsome streets and solid teak-roofed buildings, a fair-size European presence, and an air of constant movement and money being made"*.

Today's population (according to the 2010 census) is 123,800, the railway line from Yangon (260 km to the south) extends to Bagan and there is a diesel electric plant. Some recall that General Ne Win, who governed Burma between 1962 and 1988 (the country was renamed Myanmar in 1990) was educated at the local National High School, the central square displays a statue of General Aung San, in a rarely seen equestrian pose, and the main thoroughfare includes a modest shopping mall. But the "highway" connecting it to Yangon and Bagan is not exactly "well-maintained". The general atmosphere is more likely to induce a relaxed laid-back attitude than hectic living. This can be seen at the city library, a good place to read the newspapers – especially now that there are so many more of them following the new press laws – or leaf through old books in an atmosphere somewhere between that of an English club and a Burmese tea-shop.

The most significant change is the name, which is once again Pyay, recalling the old capital of the Pyu people. This was no mere toponymic decision. The future of Pyay lies in its past, in being so closely connected to the site of Śri Ksetra, roughly 8 kilometres to the east. To paraphrase Scott O'Connor, who dismissed the descriptions of the "Blue-books" by saying that *"if there be any one to whom the assimilation of such knowledge is of profit, he is respectfully referred to these sources"*, the purpose of this book *"is but to glance very briefly at the past of one of the oldest cities of Burma"*.

Historic SHWEDAUNG

by Massimo Morello

THE BUDDHA WITH GLASSES

According to a sermon delivered by friar Giordano of Pisa in February 1306, "eyeglasses" were first made by an unknown glassblower in Florence and Pisa.
Seventeen hundred years earlier, in the 5th century BC, a pair of glasses was placed on the face of a large statue of the Buddha in the pagoda of Shwedaung, a village just south of Pyay. It is now known as Shwemyethman, the pagoda of the golden eyeglasses (shwe meaning gold, myethman glasses).
King Duttabaung, the founder of Sri Ksetra, the capital of the Pyu kingdom, commissioned both the pagoda and the statue. The King, who had received the gift of supernatural sight - enabling him to also see what was hidden, just as Buddha can distinguish reality from illusion - lost his power shortly after the pagoda was completed. So, after consulting with wise men at court, he had a large pair of glasses placed on the Buddha's face, after which he regained his "sight".
In reality, the story of the ancient pair of glasses is not that simple. Because it is shot through with countless myths and characters that make up the mysterious plot of the Pyu: Deva, Celestial Beings, Naga, serpents that take on human form, warrior heroes and queens with magic powers.

As often happens, history and myth do not coincide. This is why we have to wait for the Florentine friar's sermon to put a precise date on the first pair of spectacles. History and myth would only come together later, between the 18th and the 19th century. Although discrepancies still exist due to the different ways of marking time.
In 1727, London-based optician Edward Scarlett produced the first pair of glasses with temples, thus solving the problem of how to hold them up. And in 1227 of the Burmese Era (calculated according to a lunisolar calendar drawn up during the reign of Sri Ksetra), i.e. in 1866, a pair of golden glasses with temples was placed on the face of the Buddha of Shwemyethman.
Records say that the Lord of Shwedaung, Zeyanandameik, had them made because new sects were spreading at that time that put different slants on Buddhism. Once again, a more profound vision had to be found. According to the same records, those glasses replaced an earlier pair, without specifying whether they belonged to King Duttabaung.
In subsequent decades, the glasses were replaced more and more frequently: following a theft, or to ask the Buddha to cure the eye disease of a bureaucrat's wife. It became customary to make a donation in order to change the glasses in exchange for a favour.
The moral of the tale: look beyond the Buddha's glasses…

Bibliography

Aung Thaw, U., 1968, Excavations at Beikthano, Rangoon, Revolutionary Government of the Union of Burma, Ministry of Union Culture

Aung Thaw, U., 1972, Historical sites in Burma, Government of the Union of Burma, Ministry of Union Culture

Aung-Thwin, M., 1982-3, Burma Before Pagan: The Status of Archaeology Today. In: Asian Perspectives: The Journal of Archaeology for Asia and the Pacific, Vol. 25 No. 2, 1-20.

Boriani, Maurizio & Cucarzi, Mauro, 2012. Report on the field survey condition assessment and consultations on the Pyu Ancient Cities. UNESCO, Mission reports.

Lerici Foundation, 2012, Pyu Ancient Cities; Nomination Dossier, unpublished

Gutman, P. & Hudson, B., 2005, The archaeology of Burma (Myanmar) from the Neolithic to Pagan in South East Asia, from prehistory to history, RoutledgeCurzon, London and New York, 2005, pp. 149 – 17

Guy, J., 2002, Offering up a rare jewel: Buddhist merit-making and votive tablets in early Burma in Burma Art and Archaeology, The British Museum Press, London

Hudson, B. & Terry L., 2008, Communities of the past: A new view of the old walls and hydraulic system at Sri ksetra, Myanmar (Burma). In: Journal of Southeast Asian Studies, 39/2, 269-296

Hudson, B., 2004, The Origins of Bagan. The archaeological landscape of Upper Burmato AD 1300. University of Sydney

Hudson, B., 2005, A Pyu Homeland in the Samon Valley, a new theory on the origins of Myanmar's early urban system, Myanmar Historical Commission Conference Proceedings, Part 2: 59-79 Universities Historical Research Centre, Yangon, January, 12-14

Hudson, B., 2012, A thousand years before Bagan: radiocarbon dates and Myanmar's ancient Pyu cities. Bob Hudson Field School of Archaeology, Pyay, Myanmar, & Archaeology Department, University of Sydney, "Early Myanmar and its Global Connections" Conference, Bagan, February.

Moore, E., H., 2003, Bronze and Iron Age sites in Upper Myanmar: Chindwin, Samon and Pyu. In: Soas Bulletin of Burma Research, Vol. 1, No. 1

Moore, E., H., 2011, The early Buddhist Archaeology of Myanmar: Tagaung, Thagara, and the Mon – Pyu dichotomy In: The Mon over Two Millennia: Monuments, Manuscripts, Movements. Bangkok: Institute of Asian Studies, Chulalongkorn University, pp. 7-23

Moore, E., H., 2012, The Pyu Landscape: Collected Articles, Ministry of Culture, Myanmar Archaeological Series (1), Myanmar.
Nai Pan Hla, 2011, Archaeological aspects of Pyu Mon Myanmar, Yangon.
Snodgrass, A., 1985, The Symbolism of the Stupa, Southeast Asia Program, Cornell University.
Stargardt, J.,1990, The ancient Pyu of Burma, Volume I: Early Pyu cities in a man-made landscape, PACSEA, Cambridge.

UNESCO Bangkok, 2013, Capacity building for safeguarding Cultural Heritage in Myanmar, project completion report, Bangkok.
Wheatley, P., 1983, Nāgara and Commandery: Origins of the Southeast Asian Urban Traditions, University of Chicago, Department of Geography

INDEX

- 8 Introduction *by Patrizia Zolese*
- 10 Pyu Culture *by Michele Romano*
- 14 Ancient Sri Ksetra *by Michele Romano*
- 17 The City Walls *by Michele Romano*
- 20 The Stupas *by Michele Romano*
- 32 The Early Pagodas *by Michele Romano*
- 38 Pyu Society, Sri Ksetra Museum, *by Michele Romano*
- 40 Buddhism *by Michele Romano*
- 46 Cremation *by Michele Romano*
- 54 Charles Durosielle *by Michele Romano*
- 58 Modern Excavation *by Michele Romano*
- 64 Where The Old Flotilla Lay *by Massimo Morello*
- 68 Countryside And Spirits *by Massimo Morello*
- 80 The Buddha's Prophecy *by Massimo Morello*
- 85 Back To The Past *by Massimo Morello*
- 88 The Buddha With Glasses *by Massimo Morello*
- 94 Bibliography

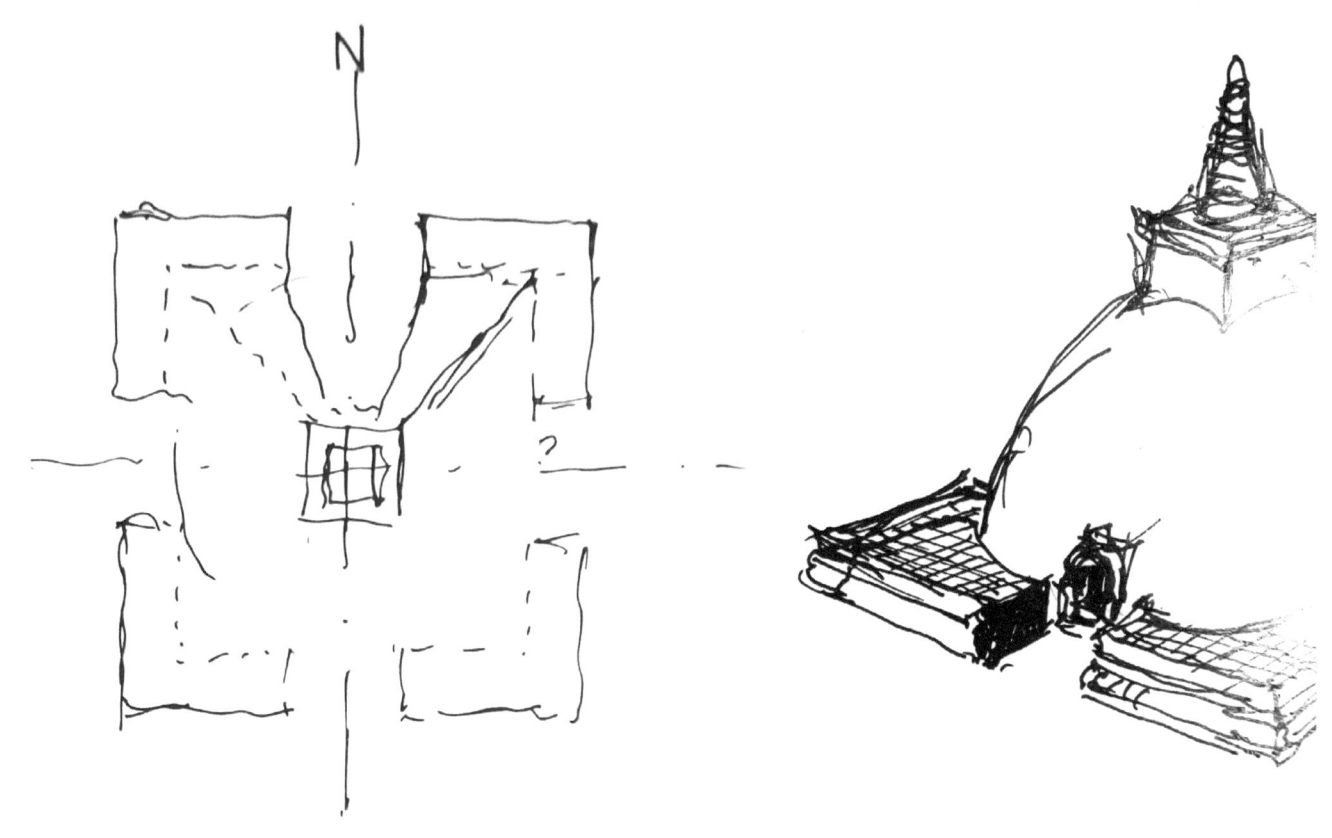

SKETCHES OF THE KHIN BA MONUMENT
(courtesy of Arch. P. Pichard – EFEO)

Sri Ksetra & Modern Pyay

This publication was sponsored by

Global Heritage Fund

Sri Ksetra archaelogical project is conducted by
Fondazione Ing Carlo Maurilio Lerici
University Polytechnic of Milano

Introduction ©2014 by Patrizia Zolese
Texts ©2014 by Michele Romano and Massimo Morello
Photos ©2014 by Andrea Pistolesi

Project Supervision by Mauro Cucarzi (Fondazione Lerici)

Sri Ksetra map published courtesy of
The School Of Field Archaeology and Dr. Bob Hudson

English translation by Vanessa Round

The publication can be licensed for printed reproduction through PadPlaces: a licensing agreement is required.
Please note that, although the publication may be licensed for free distribution, the contents (Texts and Photos) are covered by Copyright and cannot be reproduced outside the publication itself.
No reproduction is allowed in any form without the prior written consent of the authors and publisher.
Print and Electronic editions edited and published by PadPlaces (www.padplaces.com)

©2015 by PadPlaces
CreateSpace version - Available on Kindle and other on line stores
ISBN 978-88-98437-23-8

www.ingramcontent.com/pod-product-compliance
Lightning Source LLC
Chambersburg PA
CBHW040053160426
43192CB00002B/59